INSIDE
Your
Dreams

Kyia,
God's best to you always!

Mosley

SHARAY MUNGIN MOSLEY

ISBN 978-1-64468-965-3 (Paperback)
ISBN 978-1-64468-966-0 (Digital)

Covenant Books
11661 Hwy 707
Murrells Inlet, SC 29576
www.covenantbooks.com

To my parents, Pastor Herbert L. and Evangelist Helen J. Mungin—I thank you!

Thank you for applying the pressure over the years. I hear you, I heard you, and I continually thank God for you.

Love,
Sharay

CONTENTS

ACKNOWLEDGMENTS

Heavenly Father, I thank you for every word of inspiration that is written on these pages. Thank you for entrusting me with igniting the people with your promises. I thank you for letting me walk in your way and instilling in me the courage to be a light in a world so full of darkness. God, continue to order my steps. I pray your blessings upon these words and that every heart and mind shall be readily available to receive it in Jesus's name. It is so, and so it is. Amen!

Jesus Christ, you are my Sustainer.

INTRODUCTION

Inside Your Dreams Inc. is an inspiration of the Holy Spirit. I wanted to do something that would impact and reach the world. I awoke early one Saturday morning, and the idea was on my mind. I remember asking the question in my head, *What would I even call it?* At that moment, the Holy Spirit filled my mind with the name, "Inside Your Dreams."

At first, I was hesitant because I didn't think it made any sense. However, as the day went on, I continued to say the name aloud; and the more I said it, the more it made sense. On that Saturday morning in 2011, Inside Your Dreams was born. Inside Your Dreams Inc. was officially incorporated on December 7, 2011.

Inside Your Dreams Inc. is an organization where your dreams and purpose are discovered, the pursuit of goals are defined, and plans are set and executed to live your purpose-driven life. Here at IYD, I am your purpose pusher, inspirational enthusiast, and your daily hope dealer. Inside Your Dreams Inc. aspires to serve as a self-development organization that provides encouraging and motivational Christian support for those who seek to fulfill their God-given dream.

Through IYD, I share my heart, intimate conversations, and revelations that the Holy Spirit has imparted unto through the years. I pray these short devotions bless your heart and mind, as it did mine, as I wrote them.

—Blessings Flow

1

Everybody Can't Ride on Your High!

Hi there!

As I get older, I learn more and more how to appreciate the candid and impromptu conversations with my dad. Although he may not hold a four-year college degree or some big-time executive position at a Fortune 500 company, his knowledge and insight is so valuable; I can't—and I won't even—try to put a price on it. He is so full of knowledge and insight, where you can't help but to have that aha moment when speaking with him. I learn to appreciate him more and more as time passes. I guess, from all his life issues and circumstances, I can always stand to learn a thing or two from this guy, LOL!

Even I get frustrated and overwhelmed sometimes with some of the things that life throws at me. As being someone who doesn't have many friends, when I need someone to talk to, I often find myself calling home to either mom or dad! Depending on how I am feeling, that determines whether I speak to my mom or dad. LOL!

This particular day, I was in the mood to speak with Dad; Mom wasn't home anyway. Not to go into too much detail, I was feeling a little discouraged, a little lonely, and I just needed that "wisdom-ful" kind of talk. (I know that's not a word, but it makes sense for the moment, lol.) So I began explaining to my dad how I was feeling. He is not one to talk too much, but when you are in need of some advice, he listens closely and lets you get out everything you have to say. I was explaining to my dad how I was feeling very happy and blessed about all the things that were going on in my life. But somehow, I also told him how I felt alone and sad because it seemed as if others didn't share the same joy with me! (At least that's how I was feeling.) You know that feeling when you are super happy about something—whether it's a job, a new home, a new car, a promotion, or whatever else it may be! You're just happy, darn it! LOL!

So once I was finish spilling my guts and dropping a few tears in the process (I'm such a cry baby), these are the infamous words that parted my dad's lips: "Everybody cannot ride on your high." I was immediately stunned! In all the five to eight minutes that it took to spill my guts to my dad, in less than ten seconds, he parted those words of wisdom into my spirit that immediately made me feel better! Although I didn't need an explanation, he went on to say that the purpose of our blessings is not to be appreciated by others; it is to be appreciated by *you*! It is only your reactions that counts when it comes to your blessings. God is only concerned about your reaction!

Never allow the actions of others to dictate your feelings toward the blessing God has given you. Never allow the actions of others to change the way you feel about your blessings. You should never hinder or downplay your blessings because others are not comfortable with *your* blessings.

There are blessings and dreams that are ordained for each of us at a specified time! When you downplay your blessing, its the same as when someone is trying to out an unwanted flame—they smother it, stump on it, or even pour water on it. Could you imagine how God may feel to see and know that you have done that to blessings He was waiting all that time to give you?

Let me be one to tell you, "Scream it from the mountain top what God has done for you!" He said not everyone will understand your position or your blessings, but you can't let them take that away from you. You have to learn to stay focused on what and who matters most to you. Stick close to those who share that same excitement and joy as you do. I tend not to use the word *jealous* because sometimes I think to myself, there is no way possible that someone could be jealous of me or what I have when it all came from God. But what I do understand is that not everyone can tolerate what God is doing for you, especially when it is something that they also desire.

The same is for that dream, purpose, or blessing that God has given you. Your purpose, blessing, and your dream are not for everyone to understand or accept. Your dream, purpose, or blessing is not for everyone else to be happy about; but it is for you to appreciate and be happy. So as you and I continue on this journey called life, always remember to be first thankful for what God is doing.

Sometimes, just those small talks with Dad is a breath of fresh air. It helps me refocus and align myself with what's important. I hope that this enlightens you and puts a smile in your heart. Be happy, give love, and laugh lots!

Love each of you dearly,
Blessings Flow

Everybody cannot ride your high

-be appreciated by you

Thankful
to
God

2

God Is Your Preservative

Hi there!

Preservative is defined as "a substance used to keep materials or food from decay"; "inhibits decomposition." When you think of *preservative*, the first thing that comes to mind is food. There are many food items that are consumed that contain preservatives to keep it fresh for the consumer.

Each and every one of us is perfect in the sight of God. He made us in His own image; and according to the Word of God, everything He made was "good." As you and I deal with life struggles, circumstances, and disappointments, we tend to lose sight of what's important. We get distracted, and sometimes we let it over take us. But you must be reminded that you are a child of the Most High who "preserves" you. You may or may not have heard the song entitled "I Don't Look like What I've Been Through"; that song is a prime example of how God preserves His children. I'm sure that if we look like what we went through or going through right now, we would be some pretty beaten up people—LOL!

Sometimes life can beat you up and down, you encounter disappointments and distractions, and with just going through the motions, we can sometimes allow it to get the best of us. The Word of God declares, "Those that keep their minds set on me, I will keep them in perfect peace" (Isa. 26:3). You must always know and learn that in time of trouble and despair, run to your Preserver. Many may see your struggles, disappointments, circumstances, and situations; some may laugh and gossip about you; but God is your Preserver who is able to keep you steadfast. God can allow you to come out of the fire, refined as a diamond. Don't let life eat away at you because of a few downfalls, but let it be a reminder that you are getting closer.

When doors and windows are slammed shut or opportunities are ripped from your hand, always remind yourself that God is preserving you for a time such as this. The Word of God declares, "For I know the plans I have for you; plans to prosper and not harm, to give you hope and a future" (Jer. 29:11).

God will allow you to prosper within the season that He has destined for you. God will not allow things to happen before time or for them to happen too late, but He shall be an on-time God. God preserves you and keeps you through everything life has to bring, whether good or bad. It is in Christ that we find our strength and peace. For the word of God declares, "For those that keep their mind set on me, I will keep them in perfect peace" (Isa. 26:3). I encourage you today to draw close to the Father, for He made you and knows all about you; for you are His "good thing."

For some of the things we go through and encounter in life, it could have torn us down; it could have broken you; it could have cause you to become weak and feeble; and it could have even cause death. But through the preservations of Christ, He keeps us, protects us, delivers us, strengthens us, and blesses us! For all the blessings God has to give, He preserves us for the appointed time. He just wants us to hold on to His word and trust Him for His promises. God preserves us through the encouragement and power of His word; the word of God is what keeps each and every one of us secure in His will.

I encourage you today to fill yourself on the preservatives of God. Knowing that no matter what life brings your way and no matter what stumbling blocks Satan tries to create, Christ is preserving you for your appointed time.

Your dream is preserved; your life is preserved; your job is preserved; your family is preserved; that promotion is preserved; your children are preserved; your husband/wife is preserved—everything you need and want is preserved by God! He is just waiting on you to take the step of faith to trust him, for it is already yours!

I pray that this Word encourages you as much as it encouraged me while writing it!

Love ya,
Blessings Flow

3

God Specializes in the Impossible so We Know He's Possible

Hi there!

First of all, let's define some words. *Specialize* means "to concentrate on"; "to become an expert in a particular skill or subject"; "adapt"; or "invest or specify." *Impossible* is defined as "not able to occur, exist, or be done"; "very difficult to deal with"; or unable to be performed. *Possible* then means "within power of capacity"; or "can exist, happen or occur."

I'll be honest and very candid with you. Sometimes, transparency is best for particular situations. As you all may or may not know, I'm recently engaged and in the process of planning my wedding. It's a very exciting time, but it can also become very frustrating very fast, with all the planning and other stuff that goes along with it. So as I was speaking with my planner, trying to finalize the venue and decor selections, I started to vent a little because it's just so much!

As being the wonderful wedding planner she is, she reassured me that everything will work out perfectly. So when I got off the phone with her, my mind was still racing about all that has to be done. I was having a self-conversation (don't judge me, I know you do it too—LOL), and I was just saying that I wanted my wedding the way that I want it. God had already spoken and reassured me to trust Him, but as always I still worry, thinking I can do it all.

So in that moment of my self-conversation, God responded to my thought, and what He said literally stopped my whole train of thought. He said, *"God specializes in the impossible so that you can know He is possible.*" All I could say was *wow*! You may not think or believe it, but God knows and hears even our every thought, and He sometimes respond to our thoughts.

I say all that, to say this, God is omnipotent; He is omnipresent, meaning He is everywhere at the same time. God knows how we are feeling, what we are thinking, and, of course, hear what we are saying. God always has a way to reassure His people, even when we least expect it. As Christians, I think we must do a better of job of trusting God, not only with the small things but with the big things as well. I believe that it grieves Him when we say with our mouths that we trust Him but doubt Him in our hearts.

God is the Creator of the universe, and the Creator of each of us. We must believe and have faith that God only wants what is best for us. We must begin to utilize the Word of God to reassure us in the Christian walk. So whether it's your dream, your job, your family, or whatever task or circumstance that may be at hand—you must learn to lean on God's word.

I'm a firm believer that God will not bring you to something and not make provisions to see it come to pass. You must trust that with whatever God has given you, He already has a plan and a solution for every circumstance that you are to face. Even when we see it as difficult or even impossible with the natural eye, God has already made a way out of His way in the spiritual realm. Trusting God depends solely on your walk of faith and on your level of belief. I say, just look back at the difficult and impossible circumstances that you came against and remember when God made a way and allowed the best to come forth for you. Allow your past circumstances of victories to cushion your faith so that whenever you doubt, you say to yourself, "God did it then, and surely He can and will do it again."

I know, sometimes we get frustrated because we want things to happen now and we want them to happen the way we think they should happen. But this is all a lesson to trust God more for what we want and desire. Sometimes, God doesn't allow things to work for us because we are to rely on Him for the outcome. Only God can make impossible situations possible, only God can turn a no to a yes, and only God can open a closed door. Impossibilities are not our specialty—that's God specialty. And we should allow Him to do His job more often. Our job is to have faith and trust the outcome.

So, when you have come to a dry wall, an empty well, or a locked door, leave the specifics to God; you just pray and have faith that His perfect will for your life will be done. So instead of frustrating and worrying yourself with the impossibilities, just relax and have a little faith. The size of a mustard seed is all you need!

I hope that this inspires your soul and encourages you to trust God just a little more with life difficulties.

God bless, love you,
Blessings Flow

4

Like Parchment Paper

Hi there!

As I rose this morning to get ready for work, the words *parchment paper* was on my mind. I even said out loud, "Why is parchment paper on my mind?" So I kind of laughed it off as I got ready for work. When I arrived at work, I said to myself, *I know what parchment paper is, but let's see how the dictionary defines it.*

Parchment paper is defined as a nonstick surface that can withstand heat and will not burn or smoke during use in an oven.

I begin to think of life circumstances, situations, friends, family, work, and so many other things we face on this journey called life. Parchment paper is a firm example as how we should be and how we should react as we go through life's ups and downs. As I continue to mature and grow in the word of God, I realize that not everyone is against you, but not everyone is for you either. I have come to realize that everyone will not be happy about your blessings, although they will seem to be on the outside. Not everyone will be able to tolerate the favor that God has placed on your life. There may be even some friends and family who won't share the same joy and happiness with you as God propels you to higher heights. Therefore, as you grow, God continues to bless you; and when favor continues to fall upon you and your family, you must learn to be like parchment paper.

As stated, *parchment paper* is a nonstick surface that can withstand heat and will not smoke or burn. We must learn to guard our hearts, our minds, our souls, and our hearing especially. Sometimes people may offer their venomous words of so-called wisdom or their unsolicited advice because they are bitter or unhappy. However, your situation is not defined by someone else's experience.

God gave us life and life more abundantly, which means He wants us to live in the greatness that He has set before us. So when people want to kill your dreams and ambitions because they were too afraid to live their dreams or do anything about it, you must be like parchment paper and not allow those negative things to attach or take root within your heart. For the Bible declares, "Greater is He that is within me, than He that is in the World; for it is God who is greater" (1 John 4:4).

You are able to accomplish great things and be great because God has already done it. When people decide that they want to tear you down instead of build you up, you be bold and tell them what the Word of God has declared over your life, "For you [we] can do all things through Christ which strengthens you" (Phil. 4:13).

Don't get me wrong—it is very disappointing when you think people who were your friends or even family are happy for you, but actually, they aren't. So when I speak of *parchment paper*, it means not to allow the words and ideas of others to stick to you. It means to not give negativity or negative people a place within your heart. Don't allow the opinion and antics of others to become a part of who you are.

I firmly believe that if God wanted us all to be the same, He would have made us the same. Don't allow your mood, joy, peace, or happiness to be determined by the actions of others. For the Bible declares, those who keep their mind set on me, I will keep them in perfect peace (Isa. 26:3).

Sometimes, life can throw us into the fire, but remain as parchment paper for it doesn't burn or smoke while in use in an oven. If you keep yourself set in Christ, you don't have to worry about burning or smoking, but you will come out of the fire, refined as gold! For as fast as people try to speak negatively of you, you be just as fast to cast it out using the Word of God. Decree and declare that words will not stick or cause you to burn or smoke. For with the help of God, we will withstand!

—Blessings Flow!

5

Don't Let the Devil "Potty Train" on Your Day

Hi there!

The dictionary describes *potty train* as the following:

1. "trained to use the toilet";
2. "the process of teaching young children to control the timing of bladder and bowel movements and to use the lavatory"; or
3. "training a child to use the toilet for defecation and urination."

Oftentimes we allow such small things to make such a huge impact on our day. Maybe your day didn't start the way you planned. Maybe you were late to work because your car didn't want to start, you lock yourself out the house, or maybe you didn't received the great news you were expecting. Your reaction to a situation can make or break your day. Sometimes, just out of habit, we let the most detrimental words come from our mouths, for example, "This is not going to be a good day." I'm sure there are many of you who can relate.

When we allow situations to control our reactions or we let sour words leave our mouth, we open the door and directly invite Satan in. We invite him in with our words, although we don't necessarily mean them, and we invite him in with our actions because we allow what happened to change our attitude..

This is when you have invited Satan to "potty train" on your day.

Satan knows that if you can get the day started bad, you will fall into the trap and allow those detrimental words to come from your lips. You must learn to not only speak life but to recognize when things are an attack from the enemy. You must learn that when your day isn't starting how you planned, begin to speak great things about your day. For example, although you're running late for work, think about how great a day you'll be having. Even though you didn't get that promotion, think about what God has for you is for you. Although you may feel defeated, think that greater is He that is within me than he that is in the world, for it is God who is greater.

Stop affording Satan the opportunity to "potty train" on your day. Stop affording Satan first class trips of riding on your coat tail. Stop giving Satan an open door invitation. And last but not least, stop inviting Satan with your words. As the Bibles teaches, "Speak what it not, as though it was" (Rom. 4:17). Although all may not be well, speak wellness over your life and situation; although you may not be feeling happy, speak that the joy of the Lord is your strength (Neh. 8:10). Your life was not meant for "potty training." You are meant to live an abundant life.

This is not to say that trials and tribulations will not come, for they only come to make us stronger. But you have the power to speak life and control the atmosphere of your day. You have more power and control than you'll ever know because we serve an awesome God. Believe it or not, Satan has more faith in you than you have in yourself because he also knows the power that you possess. You must learn to be aware of your surroundings and control your actions. Always remember, your words shape your environment, and even though things are not always as you want them to be, they are not as bad as they could be.

Love ya,
Blessings Flow

6

Everyone Who Wants to Drink from Your Fountain Ain't Thirsty

Hi there!

This morning, I was in the kitchen packing my lunch for work, preparing to head out the door. I heard a small, calm voice say, *"Everyone who wants to drink from your fountain ain't thirsty."* I always keep a small pad and pen ready for when things like this happen. So I anxiously kept repeating it in my head until I wrote it down. Then I said it aloud, and all I could say is *wow*!

The Holy Spirit is just too wise and intellectual; He provides things to you when you least expect it—a word from God that is so fitting to what you may be going through, thinking about, or just life in general. It's always a useful word that is befitting to your situation. Think of a water fountain; it is open to the public and whomever whenever is able to get a drink of water when they want it.

These days, people do all kinds of unclean things at a water fountain. It is something that is provided for convenience in public places such as the workplaces, offices, rest areas, or playgrounds. Without regard to race, gender, age, ethnicity etc., a water fountain doesn't mind who drinks off it. Some people may get a sip of water, not because he or she is thirsty, but because it's just there.

The *fountain* in relation to your life—sometimes people can draw near to you because they see something in you. You may be a people's person, have a nice personality, successful, or people may just see you as great company and just want to be around you and a part of your life. For whatever reason, people tend to draw near to you!

Sometimes people may have underlying intentions; some people may honestly want to befriend you, and others may have hidden agendas. This is where the tricky part comes in—being able to determine who is for you and who is against you. Everyone you meet or encounter should not be afforded the opportunity to drink off your fountain. What God has placed within you is genuinely unique.

God has allowed favor and increase to be upon you and have allowed greatness to follow you wherever you go. Some draw near to you because they want that same blessing to fall upon them; but then some may draw near to use, abuse, distract, and upset you. Not all people are genuine in their actions and intentions; some just hang around to see what they can get out of the deal or what they can benefit from being around. And then some just want to see how far they can get by using you for their own growth.

People will use and abuse you, and once you have served your purpose to them, you are thrown away. Once they feel that they can't get what they want, then they no longer want to be a part of your circle.

God is your spring of living water, and your fountain flows because of Him; therefore, you must be careful that you don't allow any and everybody to drink off your fountain. If there is always giving and no receiving, eventually, your fountain will run dry. You are not public property, you are not on display, and you are not at the disposal of anyone who needs you when they call.

Don't allow people to walk up to you at any given time to use you at their disposal. Don't allow people to walk into your life and drink off your fountain just whenever they want to. We must be great men and women of standard before Christ. You draw your strength from Christ; therefore, if you allow anybody just to drink off your fountain, what would you have left to sustain you? When you allow the things of this world to consume your mind or your thinking, you are putting your fountain on display for public use.

Take your fountain off public display and pray and ask God to give you wisdom and understanding to see when people who mean you no good such as friends, associates, family, etc., are drinking from your fountain when they are not thirsty. They are drinking off your fountain because it is there; it's available and they can use it whenever they like.

Understand that God wants us to help our brothers and sisters. He wants us to uplift one another and be there for one another. We are to be our brothers' and sisters' keepers, but in no form did God say to allow ourselves to be used and abused. In no way did He say, "Make yourself available for public use, whenever people want to use you."

God wants you to be wise and recognize when the enemy is sifting you. He wants you to recognize when the enemy is trying to get you off track; and He wants you to recognize when you are being abused, distracted, and used. Ask God to give you the wisdom to know the difference. God didn't create you to be a stepping stone but a helping hand.

From your fountain sprouts favor, love, joy, peace, understanding, wisdom, promotion, increase, courage, hope, confidence, and success. Be careful who you share these things with because too much outtake and not enough intake can destroy you! Use your blessings wisely, for when a well is dry of water, it is no longer of use to those who once used it. Stay connected to the source, which is Christ, and allow Him to show you the way!

As Isaiah 58:11 says, "The Lord will guide you always and will satisfy your needs in a scorched land and restore your strength. And you will be like a watered garden like a spring who never runs dry."

Love ya,
Blessings Flow

7

Test Your Godly

Hi there!

First of all, let's define the word *godly*. The word means "devoutly religious"; "having great reverence for God"; "good"; "coming from God"; "divine"; or "have a religious character."

People will test your "godly," plain and simple! You might ask, "What do you mean by that?" People will attempt to make you lose control, make you go to a place that is ungodly. Whether it is in your actions, your words, or even your thoughts—Satan will use others to test your "godly." People can attack your character; people can attack you or do things to you that will get you out of character. Some may cause your attitude to change, some may cause you to use vulgar or inappropriate language, and, in some cases, some may cause physical harm because of what someone has done to them.

You must be able to recognize when your godly is being attacked. You can ask yourself these questions, "Is there anything that has recently tested my godly?" Did someone cut you in line at Walmart or McDonalds? Did someone cut you off in traffic on your way to work? Did you lock your keys in the car? You didn't get that promotion at work that you put in for? These are just to name a few scenarios, but there are so many things that could test our godly daily.

But it's all in how you respond to these attacks. You are to have self-control; for the Bible states, "Be ye angry, but sin not; let not the sun go down on your wrath" (Eph. 4:26). Sometimes things happen to us that is not right, and sometimes people treat us wrong or do things to us that are wrong. Guess what? We all have experienced that. But we are not responsible for how others treat us, and we are not responsible for what others do to us. But we are only responsible for ourselves, our words, and in how to react to others actions.

The Word of God declares that love covers a multitude of sin (1 Pet. 4:8). Although, someone may treat you wrong, cut you off in traffic, or jump in line at the grocery store, that doesn't mean that we have to act irrationally. I'm sure the person who did the wrong is aware that they did it. You can take the godly approach.

So the next time someone cuts you off in traffic or jumps in line at the grocery store, just say "God bless you." This will save you from ruining your day and getting upset over something you had absolutely no control over. The only control you have is in how you respond. You have the power to control your day—let your response to wrongdoing to you exemplify your godliness. Let your light shine through the darkness, for only light can cast out darkness.

Love ya,
Blessings flow

8

What's in Your Cup?

Hi there!

Psalm 23 is among one of the most popular scriptures in the Bible. Many of you know it by heart and can even recite it without looking at the words—I know I can (LOL). We read this in Psalm 23:

> Thou prepares a table before me in the presence of my enemy; thou anoints my head with oil, my cup runneth over. Surely goodness and mercy shall follow me all the days of my life and I shall dwell in the house of the Lord forever. (Ps. 23:5)

So I ask, what's in your cup?

God has made it possible that not only can we dream, but our dreams can be reality. But the reality of your dream is based on what you consist of. God has already taken care of the hard part when He sent His Son to bear all our sins and transgressions. The ultimate price has been paid so that you can live and have the abundant life that is set before you. God has set the foundation for each of us to be great through Him. Although the way has not been made straight, it has been made available. If God had made the path straight, then we would not have needed Him!

In all that we do and all that we accomplish, God still needs to be recognized as the one who made it all possible. It's not within our own will that we accomplish or obtain anything. So now that God has made it all available to us, we now have a part to do—we now have tasks set before us to accomplish. God wants to do more than we could even imagine for ourselves, but this is a two-ended deal. Yes, we ask and then we receive, but, God feels the same way; He wants to receive from us in return also.

Your cup is personal to you. It contains the recipe for your success. You must be careful whom you allow to drink from your cup, you must be careful that you don't pour out too much, and you must be careful where you place your cup. Your cup is a testimony of you—where you are going and what you are to become. Remember, God has already declared you great and victorious. You are to always guard your heart, your mind, and especially your dream. Not everyone will understand your passion and your drive; not everyone will understand your journey or your purpose. That is solely between you and God. Therefore, you are to protect your dream—cover it with prayer.

There are people out there who are ready to kill your dream, just because they didn't have the courage to fulfill their own. There are people out there who will intimidate you with defeat, just because they don't want to see you reach your full potential. And there are people out there who will kill your dream, just because they didn't have faith to trust God with theirs. Be sure that you are surrounding yourself with individuals who bring you life, add and not take away; build you up and not tear you down; and who will speak hope, encouragement, love, and faith into your spirit. Let your cup be full of those things. God has already given you the beginning, but you have to continue to add to what He has made available for you through prayer and faith.

Handle your cup with care because if you make room for neglect, that is surely what will happen. The more you stay connected with God through prayer for your dream, the more God will continue to work on your behalf. Negativity doesn't need a door to have impact in your life and on your dream; all it needs is a crack. Don't allow people to pour negativity, doubt, or fear into your cup.

When your cup is running over, it should be overflowing with success, victory, faith, courage, boldness, and positivity so that your Father in heaven will be gloried. But if you allow your cup to overflow with negativity and you allow others to suck you, it not only affects your dream, but then it begins to affect other areas of your life. Draw near to God and watch doors of opportunity open for you. You've tried it your way—now try it God's way.

Love ya,
Blessings Flow

9

You Are the Prototype

Hi there!

Prototype is defined as "the first or preliminary model of something"; "the original model on which something is based or formed"; "an original type, form, or instance serving as a basis or standard for later stages"; "the working model of a new product"; or "an early typical example."

Each of us were uniquely created in the image of Christ. God didn't intend for us to be the same, look the same, or act the same. If he wanted us the same, I figured, being as wise and omnipotent as He is, He would have done so. God also didn't intend for us to remain in the same place for too long, to become complacent, stagnant, or satisfied within our current state. God did not intend for us to begin the race and not finish. Within Christ, He wants us to be completely fulfilled beings. God intended us to grow and love prosperously through His word and to be great and successful, receiving all the many blessings that He has to give us.

You may ask yourself, "How am I a prototype?" You are a prototype simply because you have not reached your greatest potential. Although you may currently be happy and satisfied where you are, guess what? God still has more! That's amazing, right?

Think of when a new model of a car is debuted on the market. The company gives full descriptions of all the new and outstanding bells and whistles that the new car has. They paint the picture of how much more amazing the new car is versus the previous model.

In other words, they make it more appealing to the buyer. This same concept can be applied to your life's circumstances.

There are some people who are satisfied with their current state or position, and there is nothing wrong with that. They are working day by day, taking care of business and families, and they are comfortable with their life and career. But then, there are some who are just working just to get by, just trying to make ends meet. Then there are some who are just working a job because it pays the bills, and they feel they can't move on from that because they are comfortable. This is what you call the "prototype."

This world we are living in is ever changing, and things are continually evolving. You can't allow yourself to get stuck or caught between corridors of life just because you are complacent and satisfied with your current state. Just as this world is evolving, God intends for you to evolve along with it. Let's be clear, the Bible states, we are in this world but we are not of this world (John 15:19). So when I speak of *evolving*, I am referring to the Word of God and what He declares about our life.

If you remain that same model, then you are left behind. Year after year, a new model of a car becomes available; each one being uniquely different in their own way but, in some form, more advanced than the one before. So as day by day and year by year passes, you should be a much better model or prototype than you were before.

This is the same change that God wants to see in our lives. You won't be able to receive the blessings of Christ if you are complacent. Before God blesses you with something, He has to see that you are first ready to receive that blessing and that you are able to handle the blessings. God will not bless you accordingly if it is not in the right season. You are to always be continually evolving, taking the necessary steps needed to bring that dream to pass that God has placed within you.

When you become complacent, you stunt the growth of your dream. You, nor your dream are able to grow because you are not putting forth the effort to produce the fruits. Being or becoming complacent is just as bad as planting good seeds in untreated soil—there is no growth or there may be growth but the roots are shallow.

As the definition of *prototype* states, it's the preliminary model or standard for a later stage. This tells me that God definitely has much more in store for you.

God wants us to continually evolve by reading and trusting His Word. God wants us to evolve by making our request known to Him and then watch Him work wonders on our behalf. Lean and depend on Him because we can't do it alone. Being the prototype is just the basis of which God wants us to be great. For the Bible declares, "My people perish for lack of wisdom" (Hos. 4:6). You have to be willing to take the necessary steps before God can open the door. It is not in your best interest to stop where you are!

I read a quote the other day that states, "You can either live your DREAM, or help someone else to live theirs! The choice is yours." The quote rings very true! God has promised that we will be the head and not the tail—above and not beneath, lenders and not borrowers—and that we can possess the land flowing with milk and honey. The promise has been written and declared; you and I just have to walk in it.

Don't be left in your old stage because you allowed fear to settle in and gave doubt the key to your door. You must declare that this is not your end. Declare that you want more, need more, and desire more. You are a prototype in working stages; God is not through with you yet. You are continually evolving in Christ, for He is the source that will provide all the resources needed for you to be successful. Dream, dreamer!

Love ya,
Blessings Flow

10

Your Nutritional Facts

Hi there!

First off, let's define some terms. *Nutrition* is defined as "the act or process of nourishing or being nourished"; "to take in"; or "utilize." *Nutritional facts* are defined as "the labels that are placed on foods to determine the value of the food" (what is contained within the food).

Each of us were created in the image of God. We are victorious through Christ Jesus because He died so we may have life and live more abundantly. Just as foods are labeled with nutritional facts, we too are labeled. Believe it or not, we all have our own structure of nutritional facts, which either increases or decreases our value.

Take for instance a person who is not health conscious. They may eat what they want, when they want, with no regard to calories, fat intake, salt, or whatever else the food may contain. But for a person who is health conscious, this person is very careful as to what they eat. They watch their calories, and they take into consideration how bad or how good food may be for them.

This same concept can be—and should be—applied to your lives and dreams today. You are the unique vessel for your dreams. Your dreams thrive on what you feed it. A dream is just a fairy tale if there is no action/reaction put behind it. Your dream is dreamless, if you never put the effort to make it grow or give it what it needs to mature. Your dreams' nutritional facts are based on what you feed it; and whatever you feed it, it will produce the fruits of that. You cannot expect a harvest if you never sow seeds, and you cannot expect great if you sow little. You must learn to care for your dream, just as much as you care for your outer appearance. Your dream is a perception of you. You can't have a great dream in your heart with a mind full of negativity. You have to rid yourself of words that cripple you, such as *no, can't, won't, it's too late, I'm too old, would've, could've, should've*, and so many more. All these words limit your possibilities and cause your dream to go up into a whirlwind.

You have to start feeding your dreams the things you want it to produce. If you want to see greatness, then you have to begin speaking greatness and sowing these things into your dream. You have to start giving your dream your time. You have to make time for your dream—nurture it, care for it, and speak it into existence. You can't neglect your dream and expect to reap great benefits.

Begin doing things that will make your dream a reality—whether it's research, schooling, certifications, or volunteering—JUST DO IT. Your nutritional facts are based on one thing, and that's *you*! You must choose the nutritional label that your dream shall bear: faith or fear, boldness or self-pity, hope or doubt.

Think of a well-balanced diet; you also need a well-balanced dream. An unbalanced dream is the same as a beautiful home on weak foundation—it won't last. Therefore, think twice before you feed your dream detrimental helpings. Know you and your dream's nutritional facts, for now is the beginning to your future!

Love ya,
Blessings Flow

11

Amnesia

Hi there!

I am a preacher's kid; many of you know that already. I always have these deep conversations with my dad about God, faith, and the Bible. I am Daddy's girl at heart, so when I am dealing with life, I want to talk to my dad. He is a great listener. He let's me explain and get it all out and even cry it out if needed. However, he doesn't let it all end there without giving you the Word and a word of encouragement.

I remember a time when I was upset about work and just downright frustrated. I remember telling him that I keep praying, but nothing is changing. I said I felt like I was fighting for my life. He listened, but this time, he responded with a question—"Oh, you got amnesia now?" I was taken back a bit by the response because it wasn't usual for him to respond like that.

Of course, I said, "No, why would you ask me that?" He said, "Well, clearly you have amnesia because it seems that you have forgotten who God is, what He can do, and that He has the power to do it when He is good and ready."

I just let out a sigh! As the old folks used to say, "You hit the nail on the head," meaning he was right! It is necessary to have people in your life to get you back on track when it seems like you're derailing. Instead of pitying me and treating me like a baby, my dad knew exactly what he needed to do and say to get my attention away from what I was feeling. Because you know, feelings are fickle, and we can't trust our feelings all the time. Trusting our feelings sometimes can be a one-way ticket to Disaster Avenue.

My dad continued, saying, "Everything that you have prayed and asked God for you have—from your home, job, family, to finances, etc. God has blessed you above and beyond some of the things you could even ask for. So how is it that you've prayed and God hasn't answered you that you think He won't? What hasn't God done for you before to make you think He is ignoring you now? God has answered all your prayers up until this moment, so how is now that you have amnesia about who He is and what He can and will do for you?"

You know, there aren't many moments that I'm speechless; however, this talk was certainly one of them. I had no words because in that moment, I was ashamed and embarrassed. The only thing that came to my mind was, *Lord, I'm sorry!*

I pray this convinces you, as it did me! We need God and let's not forget that He loved us first!

Love ya,
Blessings Flow

12

God Majors in Minors So You Know It's Real

Hi there!

In John 14:15–31, Jesus promises the Holy Spirit, saying, "I will not leave you alone." He said the Father will give you an advocate, a helper to help you and be with you forever. Jesus said the advocate, the Holy Spirit, will teach us all the things and will remind us of His commandments.

I am a living witness that the advocate, the Holy Spirit, knows all things. He is concerned about every area of your life, even the minor stuff. In Psalm 138:8, we are taught the Lord will perfect everything that concerns you.

God wants to major in the minor areas of your life so that you know they're real so that you know the love and concern He has for you is real. Yes, God can bless us with the big blessings, but are you willing to trust Him for the small everyday things in your life? For example, the food that you should eat, where you'll get the funds to pay an unexpected bill, or even something that just annoys you—the Holy Spirit, our advocate, can handle all that and more.

For instance, I went to Walgreens the other day looking for a particular medicine, but unfortunately, Walgreens didn't have it. I said to myself, "I'll check Walmart tomorrow because Walmart has everything." Unfortunately, Walmart didn't have it either. I was beginning to get a little frustrated because I didn't want to be running around town, store to store, looking for what I wanted.

As I began to skim the shelves one last time, in my head, I said, *Lord, I wonder where can I find this thing?* The Holy Spirit immediately answered me, saying, "Go to CVS, CVS has it." Hmm! I immediately headed back to my car to go to CVS. Long story short, I got to CVS, and there it was.

I remember telling my mom about it and saying why the Holy Spirit didn't tell me this yesterday; but before I could ponder the question, He, the Holy spirit, answered again, saying, "You didn't ask." Y'all—He cares about everything, even the minor things in our lives. The Holy Spirit cares for us to have a comfortable life. The Holy Spirit is precise in what He does, if only we just ask. Something so minor such as medication, the Holy Spirit, my advocate, thought enough to intervene so that I wouldn't be annoyed or frustrated.

Reminders like these let me know that God cares and that we are not just rummaging through life looking and hoping for answers. You must ask the question, if you want the answer. I challenge you to think of the smallest thing you can think of, the smallest thing that annoys you, and ask the Holy Spirit to help you. I promise you'll get an answer. At this moment in life, I can confirm that the Holy Spirit is a carpenter, a dietician, plumber, an accountant, driver, budget analyst, a landscaper. and so much more. He is willing to help and assist with anything, if you ask! LOL!

I'm always reminded of the scripture where God says, "Try me and see" (Mal. 3:10)! I say all this to encourage you to ask the small, not-so-important questions. Ask about the things that concern you, and you'll find that it concerns the Holy Spirit as well. I pray this has encouraged your spirit.

Have an awesome week,
Blessings Flow

13

The Fingertips of God

Hi there!

You are an heir to the throne. You are of a royal priesthood. As a child of the King, you are heir to the promises of Abraham, Isaac, and Jacob. Your bloodline is rich. You are in the will. Behold, the fingertips of God are the very beginning of your life, every dream, desire, plan and hope for your life. God reminds us in Jeremiah 29:11, "'For I know the plans I have for you,' declares the Lord, 'plans to prosper you and not harm you, plans to give you hope and a future.'" He reminds us again in 1 Corinthians 2:9, "No eyes have seen, no ears have heard, nor have entered into the heart of man the things that God have prepared for those that love him." God reminds us again in James 4:8, "Draw near to God and He will draw near to you."

Just imagine—we could go through life and only experience surface-level blessings because we don't think God can provide all that we could ever need or want. At the fingertips of God is the fullness of joy, abundant life, everlasting life, and peace never ending. He's such a gentleman! In every area of our lives, it can be full and overflowing, nothing lacking. However, God wants us to welcome Him into our lives. He wants us to enjoy the fruits of our labor and enjoy the abundant life that He has set before us. However, often we want the benefits of God without being held accountable or doing the work of God. Inside the will of God, blessings are automatically assigned to you because of who you are and who you belong to.

At the fingertips of God, there is peace for worry, there is rest for the weary, faith where there is doubt, courage where there is fear, a need met for every lack, strength for every weakness, love where there is hate, hope where there is sorrow, and help when you need His hand. God is a strong tower, a place where we run to for safety (Prov. 18:10). God is our very present help in the time of trouble, and I'm inclined to think, even when I'm doubtful, fearful, scared, worried, He's still my present help!

At the fingertips of God is the complete whole, nothing-lacking antidote for life abundant. In Isaiah 41:10, God seals the deal with, "So do not fear for I am with you; do not be afraid for I am your God. I will strengthen you and help you; I will uphold you with my righteous right hand." That's sounds like a promise to me. I encourage you to reach—He's there waiting, smiling! All that you could ever imagine is already yours!

I pray this has blessed you!

—Blessings Flow

14

Act Like You Know

Hi there!

First off, let's define the word *Act*. It is defined as "to behave in a specified way"; "a thing done"; or "a pretense (a claim, or an attempt to make something that is not appear true)."

In life, we are sometimes faced with difficult and hard circumstances—"between a rock and a hard place," as some people may call it. Sometimes we try to do all we can to make a way or find provision to get out. Most times we try to take matters into our own hands instead of trusting and relying on the help of God, the Mighty One, the one who is willing and able. God reminds us in Matthew 11:28 to come to Him all who are heavy burdened so He will give you rest. God reminds us in 1 Peter 5:7, to cast all your cares upon Him, for He cares for you. God reminds us in Psalm 84:11 that He will not withhold any good thing from those who walk uprightly. God reminds us in Malachi 3:10 to try Him and see if He would not pour out blessings more than you will have room to receive.

In these scriptures, God tells us who He is—He is the Alpha and the Omega, the beginning and the end. God is and can be any and everything to each of us. God reminds us that His arms are wide open to receive us unto Him. The God of Abraham, Isaac, and Jacob is the same God unto us. So when we proclaim the love, the faith, and the strength of God, we are walking breathing ambassadors of the Father. We'll know who He is because He tells us and He shows us every day.

So when you find yourself in the funks of life, in the hard places, act like you know who God is! Act like you know you serve a God who is mighty and able. When you find yourself between a rock and a hard place, act like you know who God is. When life throws you some lemons, act like you know who God is. When your plans don't go as planned, act like you know who God is. When you have received an absolute *no*, act like you know who God is. When you can't help yourself and there's seems to be no way out, act like you know who God is.

Often we want to run to our family or friends because we like the immediate gratification of having someone to talk to. We even sometimes throw ourselves a pity party because we'd rather whine and complain instead of searching for an answer or solution. We tell everyone our problems, except God. We allow those circumstances to consume us until the brink of depression or anxiety—even sometimes to the point when we don't know who or what we are!

But we are children of the Most High, children of God, and we ought to act like it. We often do ourselves a disservice because we don't believe that God cares for even the small area of our lives. But God reminds us daily that He cares. If God cares about the birds of the air and fish of the sea, don't you know that your life's value is more than that of a bird or a fish (Matt. 6:26)? To act like you know who God is, is a position of authority and security because my confidence is within who God is to me!

God is the Alpha and the Omega.

Act like you know!

God is my rock.

Act like you know!

God is a way maker.

Act like you know!

God is a heavy-load carrier.

Act like you know!

God is a bridge over troubled waters.

Act like you know!

God is a friend of mine.

Act like you know!

God is my lily in the valley.

Act like you know!

God is my bright and morning star.
Act like you know!
God is my protector.
Act like you know!
God is a promise keeper.
Act like you know!
God is my hope for tomorrow.
Act like you know!
God is my joy.
Act like you know!
God is my helper.
Act like you know!
God is my sustainer.
Act like you know!
God is my burden bearer.
Act like you know!
God is my shield.
Act like you know!
God is my sword.
Act like you know!
God is a righteous right hand.
Act like you know!
God is spirit and truth.
Act like you know!
God is my strength.
Act like you know!
God is my peace.
Act like you know!
God is my everything
Act like you know!!

Stand in your power, stand in your authority, and act like you know you serve the author of time!

I pray this has blessed your soul! Have an awesome weekend! I love you, God loves you best!

—Blessings Flow

15

Lord, Please Help me to Wait

Hi there!

God, help me to wait in faith, as I wait on you. Help me be courageous as I wait on you. Help me live in you as I wait on you. Help me be patient as I wait on you. Help me love as I wait on you. Help me walk as I wait on you. Help me talk as I wait on you. Help me think and breathe as I wait on you. Help me to wait as I wait on you.

Lord, please help me to wait.

Help me to be faithful as I wait on you. Help me to be likable as I wait on you. Help me to be a blessing as I wait on you. Give me peace as I wait on you. Help me to be prayerful as I wait on you. Help me to be still as I wait on you. Help me to be grateful as I wait on you. Help me to be thankful as I wait on you. Help me to be joyful as I wait on you. Help me to be okay as I wait on you. Help me to be as I wait on you. Help me to be in you as I wait on you. Help me to be wise and careful as I wait on you. Help me to be understanding as I wait on you.

Lord, please help me to wait.

Help me do my due diligence as I wait on you. Help me be proud as I wait on you. Help me be renewed as I wait on you. Help me be in your way, Lord, as I wait on you. Help me be in your will, Lord, as I wait on you. Endow me, Lord, as I wait on you. Cleanse me, Lord, as I wait on you. Create in me a clean heart as I wait on you. Inspire me, Lord, as I wait on you. Help me be involved as I wait on you. Help me be attentive as I wait on you. Help me be motivated as I wait on you. Empty me of what's not like you as I wait on you. Fill me up, Lord, as I wait on you.

Lord, please help me to wait.

Help me be whole as I wait on you. Help me to live in the present as I wait on you. Help me be bold as I wait on you. Help me be encouraged as I wait on you. Help me to appreciate what I have as I wait on you. Help me to appreciate where I am as I wait on you. Help me be satisfied as I wait on you. Help me to hold my head high as I wait on you. Help me to live saved as I wait on you. Help me trust you as I wait on you. Help me be an example to others as I wait on you. Help me be happy as I wait on you, God. Help me speak faith as I wait on you. Help me sow as I wait on you. Help me be Christ-like as I was in you. Help me be Christ-like, as I wait on you.

Lord, please help me to wait.

Give me strength as I wait on you. Help me to keep trying, as I wait on you. Help me not give up as I wait on you. Help me forgive as I wait on you. Help me empower others as I wait on you. Help me help others as I wait on you. Help me overcome as I wait on you. God, just help me to wait, to be still, to be quiet in silence; as I wait on you.

Lord, Help me to wait.

Help me to wait.

Help me to wait.

Help me to wait.

Help me to wait.

As I wait on you, Lord, please help me to wait!

—Sharay M. Mosley

16

The Enemy Doesn't Like
Anything That Works

Hi there!

When something works, there is cohesiveness, togetherness, unity, hope, a bridge, happiness, purpose, strength, and meaning. I could go on and on, but when it works, there's power.

Work is defined as "to operate, to function efficiently and effectively."

So when something is working—rather, it's working for you, those around you or your community, or society, or if it just makes sense—the enemy absolutely, wholeheartedly hates it.

When you see disarray, miscommunication, malfunctions, disruption, chaos, malice, envy, jealousy, hatred, and so on, it's because something was working and the enemy couldn't stand that it was working! So he disrupts it.

The scriptures declare and reminds us in Roman 8:28 that all things *work* together for the good of them that love Christ, according to His purpose.

So your marriage, family, job, friends, career, your business, your health, your body—all of it is supposed to work. Whenever the things that are supposed to work stop working, it's time to pray. Quite frankly, keep praying on, keep praying about, and keep praying for these things before they break.

You must be able to recognize the face of the enemy to be able to stop him in his tracks. The scriptures remind us in Isaiah 26:3, "He will keep in perfect peace those that keep their minds set on

Him." In Christ is where you and I can find our peace; however, the enemy finds his peace in our misery and disarray.

If you find yourself in a situation that is no longer working but should be working, I encourage you to try Jesus. Yes, God cares, and Hs is concerned about you. In Christ, there is order; outside of Christ, there is chance! God tells us that His word will never return void. God encourages us to trust Him with every area of our life, the parts that are working and the parts that once worked and are now broken.

In Christ, things are supposed to work for our good. Even when you and I don't understand, it will still work.

I pray this has encourage you this evening! I love you!

—Blessings Flow

17

When Was the Last Time
You Made a Claim?

Hi there!

Claim is defined as "to make a demand"; "maintain as a fact"; "to state or assert"; "providing evidence of, proof of"; "something considered as one's due"; or "something that belongs to you."

When we are born into this world, we are born with no limitations. We are born with no fear, no doubt, no worry, no frustrations, or no anxiety. When we enter this world, we are completely free—free to inherit and experience the abundant life that God has promised us.

But unfortunately, as we grow, we learn to fear and worry because we allow the enemy to cause us to think different than what God has already said about us. We are sometimes taught that we can't have the desires of our hearts—you can't be successful, you can't be a millionaire, you can't be an entrepreneur. But that is the farthest thing from the truth. We allow the enemy to steal the promises that is made available to anyone who believes and have faith in God.

We become bound by worldly limitations because of what others say we can't have or what we can't do. We allow fear, worry, and doubt to become the shackles that hold us bound to those worldly limitations. Those shackles cause us to become comfortable with our circumstances and be content with not enough, and it causes us to accept less than the best of what God has for us.

So I ask this question: When was the last time you made a claim? When was the last time you made a claim over your life for every promise that God has made available to you? When was the last time you truly believed in those promises? When was the last time you made the Word of God relevant in your life?

These are some serious questions that we must ask ourselves!

God has made everything available, but we have to open our hearts and minds to receive it. God's grace and, therefore, His promises are made available each day; but you have to state your claim for those promises. Making your claim is simple—by speaking these promises over your life daily! Believe it in your heart and speak them into existence. If you read the Word of God, you will recognize that there are bountiful amount of promises that God has made for you and I. Here are some of my favorite promises that God has made available to you and me:

1. *Forgiveness*. God understands that we will fail Him daily, but I know that my Father cares for me. So when I fall short, I can sincerely ask for forgiveness, and I will be forgiven. But that doesn't mean that I take God's grace for granted.
2. *Love*. He promises to always love me, to never leave or forsake me.
3. *Brotherhood*. He promises to stick closer than a brother. I know that I can always count on Him.
4. *First*. I will be the head and not the tail, above and not beneath, the lender and not the borrower.
5. *Counts*. The last shall be first; and the first shall be last. Even when they count me out, God always counts me in.
6. *Provide my needs*. He will provide all of my needs according to His riches and glory.
7. *Fellowship*. He is a friend of mine.
8. *Grace*. His grace is always sufficient.
9. *Victory over sin*. He promises that victory is mine. He promises that all things works together for the good.
10. *Salvation*. if I believe in my heart, and confess with my mouth, then I will be saved.

The most beautiful thing about it all is that these promises are for everyone, but you have to open your heart to receive them. I pray this has been a blessing to your soul. Have a magnificent weekend!

I love you,
Blessings Flow

18

Don't Let the Devil Kick You Out

Hi there!

Do you know who you are? You are God's grand finale, His finished product, His proudest accomplishment.

That job you prayed for? God opened the door, but it hasn't been easy. That business you started? It's going, but it's so hard. That relationship you prayed for? God is working it out but still not easy. But guess what? Most times, trusting God isn't easy. It's the complete opposite of what it sounds like. Trusting God will probably be one of the hardest things you'll ever do in your life. However, through the trials and tests of trusting God, don't let the devil kick you out. Own the season you are in and embrace it.

In this season of transition, you may be doing all the right things; you're putting forth the effort, showing initiative, and being productive. However, things are still challenging and sometimes frustrating. But this is your place, the right place—right where you are supposed to be.

Fighting for your place can sometimes be hard. The enemy attacks, not because of where you are but because of where you are going. The enemy knows the path you take; therefore, don't let the devil kick you out. Don't let him kick you out of where you are purposed to be. If anything, this is a place where the enemy doesn't belong.

State your claim! What God has given to you, let no one take it from you. What God has for you is for you. That's a declaration that you should state over your life every day. It's the enemy's job to frustrate your path; it's his job to instill doubt and fear; it's his job to instill inferiority; it's his job to instill insecurity. The enemy desires to derail you, get you off track. But guess what? That's not what God promised. Where God has planted the seed is where you'll grow. Trust me—through the frustration, there is growth. Don't let the devil kick you out of your promise. Don't be so hasty to move or run; that's the enemy's way of kicking you out.

As the scriptures declare, "The race is not given to the swift, but for those that endure until the end" (Eccles. 9:11). Learn to let God do the fine-tuning. You keep moving, keep watching, keep praying!

I pray this has encouraged your soul! I love you.

—Blessings Flow

19

Get Around It

Hi there!

It's easy to get stuck, easily detoured, or thrown off track simply because the path isn't clear anymore. The path has become riddled with the frustrations of life such as worry, disappointments, fear, failure, and so much more. These situations become the norm, and you begin to accept these things as simply a part of your life. You see yourself as never getting over because no matter which way you turn, you're faced with, yet again, another one—disappointment.

However, none of these things are what Christ intends for our lives. But these very things can work together for our good. There is one thing that you must learn to do, however—*get around it*!

When we face these situations, God's word should be the guiding light, the navigation tool we must use to get through, over, and around what we face in our lives. God's word is simply our road map to getting around instead of getting stuck, buried by what life throws our way. God has a word to speak to every area of your life, in this present day. Our connection to God is through prayer. Prayer connects us to God, and when we're connected to God, we have everything.

Isaiah 41:10 tells us not to fear or be dismayed, for God will help and strengthen us and uphold us with His righteous right hand.

Psalm 55:22 tells us to cast all our cares on Him.

Roman 8:28 tell us that all things work together for the good of those who love Him.

Proverbs 3:5–6 tells us to trust in the Lord with all our hearts and lean not unto our own understanding.

I could go on and on about all the promises that God has declared for His people. His word has to become imprinted on your heart. You must believe that whatever you face; you are not facing it alone. God is always with us; He is always knocking, waiting for you to let Him in. We don't have to face life alone—God promised that. Your purpose is on the other side of all that you've encountered.

Fear can't stop you, worry can't block you, and don't let disappointment trip you. Simply learn to get around whatever life throws at you. Get around by declaring God's word daily and having faith that God can work things for your good. Through faith, what you see, is not your reality. Learn to see yourself and your life through the eyes of Christ. Create your atmosphere through the Word, that your ending will be better than your beginning—you are first and not last, the lender and not the borrower. God's word is true and as sharp as a two-headed sword. Use the Word; you have enough. Use what you got!

I pray this has blessed you as you embark on a "brand-new, shiny" week. I love you!

—Blessings Flow

20

Sometimes, Trusting God Hurts

Hi there!

The year between 2015 and 2016 has truly been a faith-defining, faith-testing year for me. It has been a year of testing and trying the faith that I so loudly declare. One thing is for sure—faith is surely easier said than done. It's easy to say that you have faith in and trust God, but it isn't easy when that same faith is tested time after time.

But what I have learned is that faith defining and faith testing is not to hurt you but to help you, to refine you, to sharpen you, to build and rebuild you, and to prune you. The way that something affects you today will not affect you the same way tomorrow. The way you react today will not be the way you react tomorrow. The way you respond today will not be the way you respond tomorrow.

Faith testing and defining challenges everything you think you know about yourself, your belief, and your faith in God. It challenges the very thing that you declare so passionately. It challenges the very idea of your faith and belief in Christ. It's one thing to say that you have faith in Christ, but it's completely different when you have to exercise that same faith with the same authority.

Sometimes—most times—trusting God hurts. The reason it hurts is because there is no negotiation with God. It's either God's way or your way; you have to make a solid decision before moving forward. You can decide to play tug of war of with God; but I can guarantee, because of experience, that you will not win. God either wants us to trust Him wholeheartedly 100 percent or not at all.

God's Word declares that He is a jealous God and that we should put nothing before him (Exod. 34:14). Therefore, when we say that we are trusting Him, that is what He expects. However, when you try to fix the problem on your own, you are ultimately saying that your way is better than God's way; you are saying that maybe God needs my help; you are saying that God doesn't know what's best and He doesn't know what He is doing. And we all know that is the farthest thing from the truth; however, that's not what our actions say.

Trusting God with 60 percent as you hold on to 40 percent is not trusting God. Trusting God with 90 percent as you hold on to 10 percent is not trusting God. Trusting God with 99.99 percent as you hold on to 0.1 percent is still not trusting God. It is not until you undoubtedly, wholeheartedly, with all your heart and might and strength, 100 percent trust God that He will move on your behalf. As the old hymn says, "Oh what peace we often forfeit, oh what needless pain we bear, all because we do not carry everything to God in prayer." We would sing that song on the youth choir growing up; however, you really don't understand the words of that verse until you begin to live your life, until you begin to experience the unpleasantries of this world.

It is not until you realize that your way isn't working until you have been tossed and turned, battered and bruised by trials and tribulations of this life, that's when you voluntarily turn it over to God. I can remember a very trying moment in my life where I told God, "You can have it all. This—all of this—is now yours to handle." It wasn't until that moment that I felt peace and a feeling of being free. It was one of the most freeing moments in my life.

However, I always know when I am attempting to pick that burden back up that I formerly released to God or when I am trying to fix a problem myself because I always get this feeling of anxiety. I become unsettled as if my peace is disturbed. I seem to feel unsure. That is when I know that I am trying to play God. And in those moments, I have to check myself. I have to rerelease and remind myself that God is in control, and I have to believe the confession of my faith.

Sometimes, trusting God hurts because, just as humans in the flesh, we think we can do it ourselves. We think that we are superman and superwoman, ready to fix whatever problems that come our way. But how many of you know and believe that you don't have to be superman or superwoman? Because God has instructed us to bring the burdens to Him. He has promised to be the burden bearer and heavy load carrier. He has promised that He will uphold us with His righteous right hand (Isa. 41:10). God has promised that He will never leave or forsake us (Deut. 31:6). God said He will lift us up so that our feet shall not strike against rock (Ps. 91:12).

As you read the Word of God, He continually promises you and me that He will always be present when we need His help. So I don't know about you, but I try every day to remind myself of His promises to me—that no matter what I face, I have an Almighty Father who is fighting on my behalf. I have armored angels protecting every step I make. I find so much comfort in that. Today, I can say that I am stronger, my faith has depth, and I have for sure a strong tower where I can hide behind the veil of the Most High. I know that my trials are not my own, but because of what I go through, I can help someone else.

I pray this as encouraged your soul today! I'll leave you with a favorite quote of mine: "When you pray, you are connected; and when you are connected, you have everything." God bless you. I love you!

—Blessings Flow

21

You Got the Bread

Be Okay with the Crumbs Until You Can Get the Bread

Hi there!

Disclaimer: I am in no way saying your current blessings are crumbs.

How many times do you think that you are so deserving of something and you feel that you should have it right now? You think to yourself, you've worked hard and have waited long enough. Better yet, you've seen others receive their great rewards for doing way less, yet you wonder why you are still waiting. Guess what, we all have to start somewhere, even if it's from the bottom.

Trust me, I've sung this tune a few times myself (LOL). I think the scripture below speaks volumes to this very feeling. (Feel free to read the entire scripture for yourself.)

> He replied, it is not right to take the children's bread and toss it to the dogs. Yes it is Lord, she said. Even the dogs eat the crumbs that fall from the masters table. (Matt. 15:26–27)

God's timing is simply not our timing; His ways are not our ways, and His thoughts are not our thoughts. The way in which we believe that we should attain and achieve things are not always the way or not at all the way God blesses us with them. To whom much is given, much is required (Luke 12:48). You must learn to be faithful with a little before God can trust you to be faithful with a lot. I truly believe that if God gives us too much too fast, we will surely mess it up. God knows our hearts, our deepest and purest desires; therefore, God must feed us as babes. God knows what we are able to handle in each area of our life and at the right time. God's blessings require maturity. There are just some blessings we are not ready to receive because we are still too immature to know what to do with them or handle them.

Start today to foster a relationship of thanksgiving. Make it a daily ritual to give thanks unto God for the things that He has already blessed you with. Be thankful for the simple things such as life, clothing (the variety), water, air that you breathe, shelter, health, your job and finances, and family, just to name a few. These are things that we are to cherish. You and I will always have aspirations and desires; however, there was once a time that we prayed for the very things that we have now. Be satisfied and content with the life that God already has given you. It's only when you become content that God can open your heart and mind to receive more. God knows what you need, and He knows what you want. God tells us to make our request known to Him; however, He also said that we must provide thanksgiving. Things may not be all that you want them to be, but it's sure not what it could be. Oh, but for grace!

Be okay with what you already have!

I love you! I pray this has encouraged your spirit! Have an amazing week!

—Blessings Flow

22

In Too Deep

Hi there!

I pray this message finds you well and in great spirits. I just wanted to encourage someone today while I also encourage myself.

A personal health issue was weighing very heavy on my heart. I found myself frustrated, seeking and wanting answers. But to no avail—I was back at square one. I found myself questioning God, *Why me? Why am I the one who has to deal with this or go through this trial?* In that moment, I was reminded of Psalm 34:19: "Many are the afflictions of the righteous, but the Lord delivers him out of all of them." I was also reminded of a devotion that stated, "God takes us through to mature us spiritually, mentally, and physically. Warfare doesn't only drain the spirit, but it also drains the body. In order to be victorious we have to be prepared, equipped with the word of God."

So while going back and forth about why this and why that, the Holy Spirit spoke so calmly to my heart, "*In too deep.*" I sort of laughed because I was like, "Isn't that a movie?"

Long story short, this rookie cop goes undercover as a drug dealer. He becomes so involved in his cover work that his fellow officers are concerned that he is getting in too deep with the cover and lifestyle. At one point, the cop does seem to lose himself in the lifestyle until he is pulled out and sent "away" to reevaluate what it is he is supposed to be doing. Eventually, he gets the job done by taking down one of the most wanted dealers in the city.

Ask yourself these questions: "Are you in too deep? Have you lost sight of the promises of God? Have you have lost sight of the

Word of God that is written on the table plates of your heart? Have you become consumed by the misery and questions of 'why me'?"

In too deep is when you forget; it's a temporary memory loss of what God has said. You know, the enemy has a way of stealing the word of God away from us when we are dealing with the frictions of this world. He rips it from our hearts so when trials come, the worry and frustrations seems to be so overwhelming.

Deep is defined as "far down"; "intense or extreme"; or "immersed."

In too deep is when we find ourselves far from what God has said. We find ourselves focusing on the problem and not the Problem Solver. We find ourselves holding the problem at a standard, instead of holding God to a standard. *In too deep* is when we find ourselves raveling over the problem, allowing it to fester into our spirit. In this moment, we are trusting the wrath of the problem over the wrath of God. And guess what? That is exactly where the enemy wants you and I to be. However, living and breathing in Christ, you and I know it's just the opposite.

As the scriptures declared many years ago, "Many are the afflictions of the righteous, but God delivers him from all of them." Yes, we may go through, but God promises to bring us through it and delivers us out of them. When you find yourself in too deep, the enemy is trying to choke the word of God out of you. However, that's when you fight using what God gave you. Use the word of God to pull yourself out of the depths of worry and despair. Will it be easy? Never. But the end result will be all for the glory of God.

I encourage you today; if you're in too deep, reach for the Word. Draw close to those people in your life who can pray for you and help you resurface again. God doesn't bring us anything that He won't bring us through. I pray you have a safe and fun weekend.

Love you,
Blessings Flow

23

Rest in the Den

Hi there!

I'm sure you're familiar with the story of Daniel in the lion's den. It's a story of faithfulness, trust, and triumph. It's a story about how Daniel prayed and was punished for displaying it three times a day. Even after being warned not to pray, Daniel still prayed without regard, committed to God. But when most people think of this story, they are reminded of how God protected him and delivered Daniel. Most times, the rest of the story in the den is overlooked. Not that it's any less important, but we tend to go straight to the victory.

So today, we focus on the rest in the den, the faith in the den, and the courage in the den (Dan. 6:1–28).

Rest is defined as "to cease movement or work"; "relax, refresh oneself"; "recover strength"; "to be placed or supported as to stay in a specified position"; "freedom"; "peace of mind or spirit"; or "to pause."

We are often faced with all sort of trials and tribulations in this life. Believing in God doesn't free us from worry or strife; however, it does promise us that He will be with us through them all. As I've often said, sometimes trusting God hurts—not as in causing physical harm or danger but trusting God often means that we have to give up what we think we want for ourselves and let God take control. It means relinquishing control and letting God take the lead. I would assume that Daniel was scared. However, his faith in God outweighed that fear, and he knew that God would take care of him. He knew that even in fear, God saw him and heard his prayers.

You and I may not be thrown into an actual lion's den today, but we face some of the same scrutiny in life. We are falsely accused, lied on, lied to, talked about, treated unfairly, and so much more. So that, my friend, is our lion's den. Sometimes, we ask the question, "Lord, why am I going through this?" or "Why is this happening to me?" And we often expect God to move immediately on our behalf. But how many of you know that God doesn't move on our time? God commands us over and over to trust Him, that He will not forsake us or leave us; but if we put our trust in Him, He promises to deliver us from the hands of our enemies.

Finding and acquiring rest in the den is critical to your survival and your faith. Finding rest in the den means that although you don't see a way or what you see doesn't match what God says He will do, you will find rest that the God of Abraham, Isaac, and Jacob will deliver and protect us. Finding rest in the den means that although you don't see it yet, you know that God is working. Therefore, those things that come up against you—those people and their words that come up against you—God will allow His angels to shut their mouths. God will allow His angels to destroy every word of condemnation that comes up against you. God will allow every infraction to be swallowed up. Finding rest in the den is knowing God will work it out and always for the good. Rest in the den is feasting on the word and realizing that God may allow it to come against you, but it won't overtake you; it will not stick or materialize. Resting in the den is imperative to the victory! As the Bible states in Psalm 91:9–10, "If you say the Lord is your refuge and you make the Most High your dwelling, no harm will overtake you."

So just as God kept Daniel, gave Daniel rest, and delivered Daniel—God can and will do the same for you. I pray and strive each day to be like Daniel, to have perpetual faith, knowing God is always able, if we let Him. I pray this has blessed you. I pray you have a beautiful day. I love you! God does too.

—Blessings Flow

24

Take God Right

Hi there!

If you give Him the heart, He can rule both soul and body. It's a favorite of my Dad—God wants all of you. I'm inclined to think God feels cheated when we don't fully invest in Him and apply His Word in every area of our lives. Most people often take God according to the need; but when the need is fulfilled, we place Him back on the shelf until another need arises.

Take God right.

When you get sick and the doctor prescribes medications, you take your meds according to the directions prescribed. In order to get well or achieve a certain outcome, we follow those medical directions to the tee.

Take God right.

So when we desire the Father to be a part of our lives and we want Him to order our steps, we lay it all before the throne because He does say, "Bring all of our burdens to Him," right? We are ultimately saying, "God, I need you, so lead me." But as God begins to order our steps and things are going well, somewhere along the line, we decide that since things are going well we think God needs an assistant. So you start butting in, telling God what's best and overriding His decision, because things seem to be going so well. Then God decides to back off because you don't seem to need Him because all of a sudden, you know what's best.

Take God right.

So as you begin to prescribe your own directions to your life, you notice you aren't well. Things that once worked aren't working; things that were easy are now complicated; where favor once was is now filled with frustration. God's grace is still sufficient, but you've moved out of His will into yours.

Take God right.

Your symptoms of frustration, anxiety, and being overwhelmed are now resurfacing because you unprescribed to your medication. You decided, at some point, the Author of time was mistaken; He somehow didn't know what was best; He moved too slow; He didn't seize opportunities that you thought were amazing. He closed instead of opened your best opportunity. All because you didn't take God right.

God is jealous, and He doesn't share—there's no in between. He's either wants all or none. Again, His grace is still sufficient, He still loves you, but He didn't move; you did. You see, taking God right or not at all has its consequences. Taking God right doesn't free us from worries or frustration but rather gives peace as we go through. Taking God right frees you of that load.

As prescribed, God came so we may have an abundant life. As prescribed, He died so that we may have access to the tree of life. As prescribed, He said, "Come to me all who are heavy laden, and I will give you rest." As prescribed, He took our place. As prescribed, He said, "Try me and see if I won't pour out unto you." As prescribed, it is written, but you must follow.

I hope this opens your heart to Him. Let him lead you.

I love you,
Blessings Flow

25

Good Thing

For the Lord God is a sun and shield; the Lord
bestows favor and honor; no good thing does he
withhold from those who do what is right.

—Psalm 84:11

Somebody say, "Good thing!"

God is just that good. It's an amazing feeling to know that we serve a God that delights in
blessing His children. He is a rewarder of those
who trust Him. (Hebrews 11:6)

Good is defined as desired or approved of; morally right or righ-
teousness; suitable or fit; agreeable; morally excellent; virtuous; ben-
eficial or worth it.

Now, that's the character of God! Good thing we serve a God
like this!

How many times have you said that saying, "Good thing"? You
say it in reference to something that could have happen in spite of.
For example, "Good thing I had cash because I would not have been
able to pay for that"; or "Good thing I ate before coming because
dinner is being served late"; or "Good thing I have my umbrella
because I didn't know it was going to rain."

Somebody say, "Good thing!"

For the Lord delights in His people; he
crowns the humble with victory. (Psalm 149:4)

Somebody say, "Good thing!"

God takes pleasure in pursuing you and blessing you. It is His desire
that above all else, we prosper and be in good health (3 John 1:2). We
know that God's timing is not our timing, and His ways are not our ways
(Isaiah 55:8–9). Therefore, when you ask for anything, God delights in
doing it for you. However, if it doesn't happen expeditiously, that doesn't
mean that God says no, it just means not yet. God knows what we can
handle in every moment and day of our lives. God knows that if He
gives you certain things prematurely that you will mess it up. God knows
in what seasons to bless you with certain things. God is a timely God,
a God of order and precision. God wants to ensure that when He does
bless you with the things you ask for, that you can maintain them and no
one can destroy them. God wants to ensure that your blessing is used as
a testimony, and He gets the glory. God wants to ensure that you know
it was only God that gave you that good thing. Therefore, when it does
happen, you'll find yourself saying, "Good thing I waited on God," or
"Good thing God didn't give it to me when I wanted it."

The good thing about God is that he already knows that. God
doesn't make you wait to hurt you, He make you wait to assure
you—to build perseverance, character, and most of all, your faith.
Good thing we serve a good God—a God that looks at your best
interest when you can't see clearly or beyond your carnal desires. In
all that's good and pleasing to God, He wants to bless you with it. If
it's good and good for you, it's yours; however, in faith, we must wait
sometimes for the proper season to reap it. Your "good thing" lies in
your faith. I am reminded of a quote I saw a few years ago, "If it ain't
good, God ain't finish." Because everything God created, He declared
it good when He was done. I pray this encourages you to stay the
course and stay connected. God is listening, and in due time, you
shall reap the harvest. I love you, but God loves you best!

—Blessings Flow

26

Like Grace

Dress like Grace
Love like Grace
Forgive like Grace

Oh, but for Grace.

Hope like Grace
Live like Grace
Believe like Grace

Oh, but for Grace.

Show up like Grace
Give like Grace
Act like Grace

Oh, but for Grace.

Move like Grace
Respond like Grace
Listen like Grace
Shine like Grace

Oh, but for Grace.

See like Grace
Walk like Grace
Talk like Grace

Oh, but for grace.

Laugh like Grace
See like Grace
Answer like Grace
Forget like Grace
Enter like Grace
Teach like Grace

Oh, but for Grace.

Hope like Grace
Learn like Grace
Hear like Grace
Feel like Grace
Understand like Grace
Win like Grace

Oh, but for Grace.

But He said to me, my grace is sufficient for you, for my power is made perfect in weakness. Therefore, I will boast all the more gladly of my weakness so that the power of Christ may rest on me. (2 Corinthians 12:9)

27

When God Shows You You're Ugly

The character of God shows in His Word and His works. The character of God shows in each waking moment that you see a new day, take a breath, makes ways out of His way, and blessings that He bestows exceedingly. Genesis 1:27 tells us that God created mankind in His image, and when He finished, He said it was good. God created mankind to mirror the heart, mind, and spirit of God. God wants us to be like Him, look like him, love like him, act like him, and respond like him. And all these things are good, right!

So what happens when you don't look like Christ, respond like Christ, act like Christ, or love like Christ? It's in those moments that God shows you how ugly you are! That hurts, I know. Anything less than the image in which Christ made you is ugly. You might say, "I am human, and I have faults and I make mistakes and I am not God." And I would say you are absolutely right; however, there is grace for that. As Christians, we are not to live, act, respond, and love like the world. We are men and women of standard—a light that it set upon a hill that cannot be dimmed.

Often, you may find yourself in situations where someone doesn't treat you well, or respond to you well. However, you are not responsible for how others treat you, but you are indeed responsible for how you treat or respond to others. In those moments you are displaying your godly character. When you respond as others do, you are showing your ugliness. Let's be honest, we all have a little ugly in us. However, God teaches us to cover the ugly in grace and forgiveness. God teaches us to forgive the ugly and indiscretions of others just as He does for you and me.

It's impossible to be in the likeness of Christ and remain ugly. Grace and forgiveness are for everyone, but especially for those that shadow the character of God.

God shows us in an array of ways how ugly we can be. We are ugly when we harness unforgiveness, unkindness toward others and ourselves, when we aren't friendly, when you are sharp with our words, when we aren't gentle, when we don't offer a helping hand when you are able to do so, and when you can go the extra mile but you don't because of selfishness—just to name a few.

In the shadow of God, we must sometimes do what we don't want to do; we must forgive even when it seems impossible, and say sorry when we are wrong. In the shadow of Christ is where we learn the likeness of Christ—when we learn the character of Christ and learn to live, breath, and have our being. In the shadow of Christ is where our own character is refined and polished. It's where Christ grooms us to be more like Him, set a part. In the shadow of Christ, is where God stretches us to go beyond carnal feelings, where He teaches us to respond in love, even when love isn't shown. In being like Christ, it requires us to love more and forgive often. It requires us to draw on Christ rather than misplace our expectations.

I pray this encourages you to examine yourself. I pray that you ask God to show you the ugliness of your heart and leads you to realign yourself with the character of God. I love you, but God loves you best.

—Blessings Flow

28

When God Gets Mad

I'm sure you are familiar with the story of Jonah in the Bible. If you are not, I encourage you to read the story. The plot of this great story resonates with so many areas of our lives today. God reminds us in Hebrews 13:8 that He is the same yesterday, today, and forever. So we know God doesn't change; however, we do. We are human, fickle and carnal, but God knows that too. What I find most interesting about this story is that God knew that Jonah was going to run from what He called him to do. However, God didn't chase Jonah, but he allowed Jonah to face some very difficult decisions because he was disobedient.

Disobedience is defined as failure or refusal to obey rules or order in authority; neglect to obey.

Romans 8:7 says the mind governed by the flesh is hostile toward God; it does not submit to God's law, nor can it do so.

So when you are disobedient to the will, purpose, and plan of God, you are hostile toward God. You can't say you choose God, but don't follow what He says. And yes, I know, God lovingly forgives us all, but that doesn't give permission to continue in wicked ways.

God told Jonah to go to Nineveh to prophesy its destruction; however, Jonah didn't want to go. I don't know if it was out of fear, worry, or distress, but Jonah was out of there. Lol! Jonah ran, plain and simple, in hopes that God would change his mind or choose someone else. But that's not how God works. God's choices and decisions are always well directed and sought for His own purpose and glory. Jonah ran long and far, but it wasn't long enough or far enough.

Instead of chasing Jonah, God made Jonah's situation uncomfortable and almost unbearable. God let Jonah get far enough to think he was unseen. Jonah found rest and refuge in the bottom of ship, and he fell asleep. God was not going to let Jonah get off that easy, so He had a plan for His plan. As the ship began to sail, God sent a storm to disrupt Jonah's plan.

God allowed Jonah's plan to become scary and difficult. I don't know about you, but I would sure be frightened if I was on a ship that went through the storm that Jonah endured.

When God gets mad, it not always obvious. It's not always fire or opening of the earth or unleashing venomous snakes. Sometimes, God's anger is the result of your own actions and disobedience. In the words of the old folks, when you play with fire, you will get burn. Sometimes the anger of God is the pain of your consequence. The story goes on to say that the crew was in distress because they didn't understand the storm because they had taken that trip so many times without worry. Jonah knew the storm was God's reaction to his disobedience. His disobedience put other people's life in danger; his disobedience caused distress for others. This also shows that the results of disobedience doesn't just effect you, but those you love and others around you. The severity of disobedience causes a ripple effect, something like an earthquake, others feel it to.

Jonah knew he had to do something, so he told the crew to throw him overboard, and they did. Jonah was swallowed by a fish and eventually spit on the shore. You see, God's wrath could have killed Jonah, or God could have just used someone else. But God understands the purpose of the life his has given, and he understands the importance of his plan for his people. God's plan is for the benefit of his people and for his glory. When God gets mad, it may show up in the most inopportune way. The storm in your life may not be an actual storm, but it could be distress in your family or on your job. It could show up as challenges in your finances or your marriage. Sometimes, God just allows the natural occurrences without even touching you. He allows these heightened moments to allow us to see the error of our ways. God uses these moments to get our attention, to show his power and love for us.

Hebrews 12:6 says the Lord disciplines those he loves. God's wrath is a portion of discomfort and love all wrapped in one. God loves you, you know this! I pray you understand that God loves the best of you and wants only the best for you. Stay encouraged.

—Blessings Flow

29

Self-Agenda

God has been tugging at my heart lately, and I felt compelled to talk about this. The "self-agenda" is dangerous, damaging, deceitful, and deadly. It was not intended for you to do it alone, neither should you want to do it alone. God intended that you would want Him to help you, direct you, and even carry you. This agenda for "self" is being pushed everywhere you turn, from the pulpit to the pit. It's being dressed up as something to be sold on shelves to the highest bidder. This is a weapon of destruction that so many are falling for. This is a false agenda, meant to make you believe that your life fulfillment comes from you. It leads one to believe that you are self-made, self-motivated, or even self-sufficient.

Self is defined as inner fulfillment; by one's own effort, by its own action; inbreed.

Anything self says it's, "I did it myself in my own strength".

Now, let me clarify before you get your panties in a wad. In no way am I saying not to take care of the physical body. However, what I am saying is that you cannot do this life alone, merely relying on oneself. There are limits to your flesh, and ultimately, your flesh is deceiving and self-serving.

I'm sure you've heard them too:

- Self-care
- Self-motivation
- Self-hope
- Self-help
- Self-love

If you are merely relying on yourself to do anything, you are in for a big surprise. This agenda is misleading, and not practical for Christian living. In acknowledging "self" for things that only God is capable of doing is a lie. You've just lied to yourself, and to God.

The self-agenda says, "I can take better care of myself than God can. I know what I want and need, surely God doesn't know that."

Grace says, "That is a lie."

The self-agenda says, "Certainly, I can love myself better than God can. I know myself, and I know what I want."

Grace says, "That is a lie."

The self-agenda says, "I am self-sufficient. I am able and capable to do it for myself. I am able to maintain and keep myself afloat. I am able to get it done for myself, by myself."

Grace says, "That is a lie."

The self-agenda says, "I don't need God's help or anyone or anything to help me. I can help myself. It says God doesn't know what I need, but I do. The self-agenda says, I look within for my motivation. And I know what you might say. Well, the Bible says to encourage myself. Yes, yes it does, but you're forgetting one part. It says to encourage yourself in the Lord [1 Sam. 30:6]. It says that faith comes from hearing the Word of God. So, yea, that still requires help from God's Word."

Self cannot do a thing for self without love and instructions from God. Proverbs 16:9 reminds us that the heart of man plans his way, but the Lord establishes his steps. In this, God is reminding us that "you need me, and I want you to need me, but I won't force myself on you." In Philippians 4:13, it says, "I can do all things through Christ which gives me strength." So what does that mean? It means that you are on borrowed strength. Even when you don't invite Him in, or ask Him for help, you are still on borrowed strength, help, care, hope, and love. God is good like that. Even when you do like Him or love Him, He still likes and love you. His grace reigns on the just, as well as the unjust. God's love is given without expecting anything in return; however, He desires that you come to Him. So as you live, I pray that when you attempt to rely on self, that it prompts you to call on the One that has all power, the One that loves you unconditionally and desires for you to prosper and be in good health. Remember, God is good like that. I pray this has encouraged your soul. I love you!

Love you,
Blessings Flow

30

Trace Your Steps

Hi there!

Frustration, doubt, and anxiety are sometimes all too familiar. Dealing with life circumstances can bring on these feelings, but God reminds us to not act like we have no hope (1 Thess. 4:13).

Every now and then, we need to be reminded who we are and whose we are. The enemy can't change what God has orchestrated; however, he seeks to distort your view and change your focus. This is how we fall short and get detoured off the path that God has destined for us. Despite this, God is always waiting, willing, and lovingly with open arms to always—*always*—receive us back unto Him. I came across a quote that was so befitting of this and it states, "Trust Him. He's carried you this far, hasn't He? Don't you think He could carry you any further? Trust Him."

What little words but packs such a powerful punch! In Psalm 138:8, we are reminded that God will perfect that which concerns us. We are also reminded in Matthew 28:20 that God is with us always, even until the end of time. If you take a moment to trace your steps, you will see that God has been right there with you, guarding you, rerouting you, and deterring you from anything that wasn't good for you.

Even if God allowed you to go through a storm, it was for a lesson, a fulfillment that was necessary for our life. Often, we focus on the things that we don't have and forget to be thankful for what God has blessed us with. When you find yourself in this rut, I encourage you to trace your steps. You may not have everything you want, but you have everything you need. Everything may not be perfect, but thank God they aren't worse. There's always something to be thankful for. Things could always be worse than what you think your worse is! Trace your steps.

At every point of triumph and every point of failure, God was right there. In Psalm 23, it states, "Yea thou I walk through the valley in the shadow of death, I will fear no evil. For you are with me; your rod and your staff comfort me." In your darkest valley, God has the power to pick you up and carry you; however, He allows you to walk because God must teach us to be strong and not to fear. God must teach us to be bold. God must teach us to walk by faith and not by sight. God teaches us that by allowing us to walk, as He walks with us. Trace your steps.

God is not absent or unaware, but God must show us that He is there instead of always telling us. Just as a baby learns how to walk, they may fall a few times before gaining balance, but they don't quit. Faith is persistent in the pursuit of what God's Word tells us and what He has for us. Anytime you need a reminder or you're not sure if God is there for you, trace your steps. You'll find that He's been there all along, destroying hurdles, bulldozing roads, creating new roads, protecting you from the enemy's plots, and being a bridge where there are holes. Trace your steps.

God is a God of rearranging, especially when we think we know what is best. God isn't going to let you hurt yourself; He will reroute, if necessary. Just trace your steps.

I pray this has blessed your spirit! Hope you're having an amazing day!

—Blessings Flow

31

Traffic Control Your Thoughts

Hi there!

Often, while trying to get to sleep, it's hard to quiet my mind. My thoughts are often racing from one thing to another. It's not necessarily anything in particular, but I go through a series of meditation techniques to calm my mind. My body is ready to rest, but my mind jumps from one thing to another. It's annoying because I find myself lying in the bed for hours before I get to sleep.

There are instances where I just get back up and watch TV until I get extremely sleepy and can't take it anymore. LOL! However, last night was a little different. I was trying to get to sleep, but I could tell that my mind was racing. But this time, the Holy Spirit intervened in a gentle voice, saying, "*You need to traffic control your thoughts!*" I immediately knew what God was saying—no explanation needed. LOL!

An air traffic controller has a really important job! They are responsible for monitoring and directing the outgoing and incoming traffic of the airport. They ensure the safe landing and takeoff from an airport; they facilitate the safe and orderly movement of airplanes as the enter and exit the airports to ensure there aren't any collisions. Just as an air traffic controller controls the airways of the sky, I too needed to control of the airways of my thoughts. I needed to be conscious of what I watch, listen to, or even the conversations that I partake in. The brain is the control center for the body; the brain is where signals are sent from and to, to ensure that your body operates as efficient as possible. Therefore, I need to traffic control the thoughts that I allow in my head because eventually, what you don't control will control you.

My thoughts need to be as efficient and precise as an air traffic controller. We must learn how to arrest thoughts that are not of God, thoughts that are time consuming and wasteful. We must learn how to control what we allow in and through our thought-processing center. Allowing your thoughts to run rampant, eventually, a collision is bound to happen. Those collisions are just as detrimental as an actual aircraft accident. Those rampant thoughts cause indecisiveness, depression, anxiety, restlessness, stress, toxicity in relationships, and it will begin to spill over into every other area of your life—sometimes affecting those close to us as well!

Traffic controlling your thoughts begin by knowing who you are in Christ and what He says about you. God's Word says, "If you abide in me, I will abide in you" (John 15:4). Traffic controlling those thoughts begins by arresting any and all thoughts that don't align with the promises of God; whether big or small. Allowing the smallest of those insufficient thoughts to run rampant, they can take root; they begin to make your mind and your thoughts their home. And before you know it, you're restless, tired, irritated, and you don't know why.

Some of the many ways I'm learning to traffic control my thoughts are through prayer and meditation. At the first sign of insufficient thoughts, I say a small prayer, "Abba, I belong to you." I repeat this short prayer as many times as possible until I feel the thought is gone. I sometimes even use the old faithful, "The Lord rebuke you, in Jesus's name." Pay attention. Focus and be on guard to recognize when your thoughts are running rampant. I encourage you to practice using techniques that will help you take control of your thought life. As the Word of God declares in Proverbs 23:7, "So a man thinks in his heart, so he is." So, yes, you can become what you think, but we want those thoughts to be Christ driven, with power and purpose.

I pray this has encouraged your soul today! Hope you have an amazing rest of the week. I love you, God loves you best.

—Blessings Flow

32

Your Transmission

Hi there!

First off, let's define some words. *Transmission* is defined as "the mechanism in which power is being transmitted from the engine to the wheels of a car"; "power is transmitted from the engine to the tire axles"; "the transmission of power"; or "the transmitting of radio waves from station to station."

I had an interesting weekend. I was in distress, okay? Nevertheless, I am here to talk about it, so I am grateful. Life can be crippling sometimes; it can hit you with some hard blows that the last thing you can think about is praying. However, God has blessed me with an amazing village. I always encourage people to get or have friends and family who can pray and intercede for them in times of distress. Those are your people, and they are priceless.

I had a revelation, and I just had to share. You know what a transmission is right? You know, that thing besides the engine that helps your car to move. Most of us know the transmission is an important part in the operation of any vehicle. Well, you also know transmission occurs with radio or satellite frequencies. For instance, when you're trying to find a good radio station on a road trip; you need a good frequency.

Go with me; I promise it's going to bless you!

If you've ever had issues with your car's transmission, then you know that's a major problem. I don't care how well your engine is working; if your transmission stops, everything else stops too. For the transmission to work properly, the lines and the filters must be clear and clean. When your transmission filter is clogged, the transmission can't efficiently transmit its power. It then causes many symptoms such as bad fumes, smoke, noises, and leakage, to name a few. Ultimately, if maintenance isn't done, the transmission will eventually stop.

I'm inclined to believe that the transmission is to the car as God is to our hearts. The same way the transmission flows the power of the engine throughout the car, that is the same way God transmits His power to our hearts for us to operate in and through Him. Let's just say, I was having some major transmission problems this weekend.

I allowed the enemy to infiltrate my mind and heart on an issue that is rather close to my heart. I fell vulnerable to the lies and manipulation of the enemy, although I know what God has told me. My transmission lines were clogged because I allowed the manifestation of the enemy's word to infiltrate my heart. God couldn't transmit His words or love to me like He normally does because my lines—my heart—were being filled with trash. The lies of enemy are just that, trash. The enemy comes to do three things: kill, steal, and destroy. There is no good thing that comes from him (John 10:10).

God desires clean and clear lines to operate freely in your life. God needs open and clear frequencies in order to plant His words into your heart and mind. You can't embody the spirit of fear and faith at the same time; just as you can't embody light and darkness at the same time. With God, we must choose—choose to have faith in the face of adversities or choose to punk out to fear. God's Word is only as good to you as the soil you plant it in.

We have some work to do. God needs our absolute faith. It's time to clear those clogged lines of doubt, fear, worry, and anxiety. How can God freely operate for you and through you when your lines are filled with trash? There is no way God can get a clear message to you when you're filled with everything, except Him. God has His own special way of talking and dealing with each of His children. God wants your heart. God wants you to sweet surrender. God does not leave you hopeless but hopeful; not fearful but fearless!

Listen, shout unto God! I could dance like David right now! I hope you catch that Word. I pray this has blessed your spirit. Have an awesome day!

—Blessings Flow

33

Oil Change

Hi there!

If you have a vehicle, you know and understand the importance of getting an oil change. An oil change is the removing of old oil in your engine and replacing it with fresh oil. This process ensures that your car engine has adequate lubricant to operate well. We've all heard the horror stories of what happens to cars when they don't get oil changes—they blow the engine, and the car stops working completely.

What if I told you that your physical and spiritual body works the same way? It's impossible for you to operate day in and day out with the same oil. In the Lord's Prayer, it states, "Give us this day our daily bread." This tells me that every day my eyes open, I need to request my daily bread from the Father. I know you've heard the saying that you can't pour from an empty cup. That means, for you to give yourself, you must be filled first. Psalm 23 states, "My cup runs over." This means what's in the cup is for you but what runs over is for you to give. There is a prerequisite to starting each day, welcoming God into the day because you don't know what each day will bring or what you shall face.

If you're like me, I tend to compound my feelings. I want to be and appear strong, so I compact my feelings without expressing them wholly. The problem with that is over time, those compacted feelings and emotions become too much to bear, and without notice, they begin to overflow. Then boom—all at once those feelings from months ago come out and you have a meltdown. This is exactly what happened to me, so I know from experience.

This is not the will of God. God wants you to come to Him frequently for your spiritual oil change, your spiritual maintenance. God wants you to operate smoothly and efficiently in Him. You can't allow your engine, your heart, to become overturned in emotions and feelings that you forget to check in with the Father. You were not meant to do this life alone. God said in 1 Peter 5:7 to cast all your cares upon Him, for He cares for you. God desires that you bring all your worries, cares, concerns, feelings, and emotions to Him. God does not delight in your misery, but He wants you to know that He cares.

This spiritual oil change requires that you empty yourself of those cares, every feelings of fear, doubt, and worry unto God. It requires that you empty yourself of the lies that the enemy has fed you; it requires that you empty yourself of everything that's not of God. It requires that you empty yourself of you. It is only then that God can refill you with fresh oil. Every now and then, we require a renewing of the mind and spirit, reminding yourself of every promise and blessings that God said is already yours. You need the fresh oil of the Holy Spirit to operate at full capacity. The fresh oil of the Holy Spirit covers and heals the hurt and bruises of this life. Without your spiritual oil change and maintenance, you can't use what God has given you, and you can't be who God has called you to be. So as you face life's challenges, I encourage you to get your oil change. Allow God to refresh His anointing on your life. Allow God to remind you who you are and whose you are. God has given us the opportunity to live an abundant life, and I pray you take full advantage of it. God loves you, and so do I!

—Blessings Flow

34

Love by Example

Hi there!

Lord knows dealing with people can be hard and even sometimes exhausting. Sometimes, people can say and do things to you that can be hurtful and even detrimental to the relationship. In those times, you may want to cut them off or distance yourself from them, but that's not always as easy as it sounds. Depending on who those people are, you can't always cut them off or distance yourself when you want to.

The Word in 1 Corinthians 13:4–7 tells us this:

> Love is patient and kind; love does not envy or boast; it is not arrogant or rude. It does not insist on its own way; it is not irritable or resentful; it does not rejoice at wrongdoing but rejoices with the truth. Love bears all things, believes all things, hopes all things, endures all things.

Peter 4:8 adds, "Above all, keep loving one another earnestly, since love covers a multitude of sins."

I had just arrived at work, preparing myself to get started with my workday, and the Holy Spirit dropped into my spirit, "*Love by example.*" Little did I know, God was preparing me for something to come later in the morning.

I was doing my usual Facebook scroll and came across a Facebook post of a family member that was very disheartening; it was hurtful—spiteful, to say the least. I was angry by what I read because I had just had a conversation with this person earlier in the week, trying to encourage them. I felt that I had thrown my pearls to swine. I immediately called my mom to talk me through it because, you know, that's what moms do.

After talking with my mom, she reassured me that everything would be okay and that I need not worry myself about what others say or do—and she was right.

After having the conversation, I was immediately reminded of the word the Holy Spirit gave me that morning, "Love by example." You know because when someone hurts you or offend you, the first course of action is to cut off and remove yourself from the situation. I'll be honest, that's exactly what I wanted to do. However, God was preparing me for that offense before it even happened by reminding me to love by example.

God loves us unconditionally, no matter how many times we mess up. God loves us without condition and without strings attached. How many times have you and I offended God with our actions or thoughts? How many times have you hurt God's feelings because of disobedience? It's way more than any of us could ever count. So God wants us to love the same way.

Yes, it's hard, but it's necessary. I'm not saying to lie down and let someone mistreat you, but in Matthew 18:22, one of the disciples asked Jesus how many times we should forgive. Jesus replied, "Seventy times seven." I'm sure that Christ forgives us even more than that. Even in our offenses, God loves us and forgives us more times over than we deserve; therefore, we should offer our sisters and brothers in Christ the same grace.

Even when it's not easy, the Father is there to help purge our hearts so that we can see the bigger picture. God loves you, and God wants you to love like Him—love by example. I pray this has blessed your spirit.

I love you,
Blessings Flow

35

God, I Don't Know How, but I Know You

We read in Acts 1:7, "Jesus replied, 'It is not for you to know the times or seasons that the Father has set in His own authority.'"

You ever found yourself in an uncomfortable situation and didn't know or see a way out? You tell yourself, *What I see doesn't look good and how I feel is even worse.* Have you ever told yourself, *It doesn't feel good, God, but I know you. It doesn't look good, God, but I know you*? You say, "God, I know what the doctor said, but, God, I also know you. I feel the pain, God, but I can also feel you. I'm worried, doubtful, fearful, but I know God. I don't know where, when, or how, but I know God."

I can imagine Moses at the Red Sea, stuck between a rock and hard place—the Red Sea before him and pharaoh's army behind him. God told Moses to use what he got, so he used his rod and commanded the sea to part. Moses didn't see a way out, but he knew God.

I can imagine Daniel in the lion's den, scared, perplexed, not sure of what might come of him in this place. But Daniel prayed to the one he knew who could deliver him. Daniel didn't know how, but He knew God.

I can imagine the three Hebrews boys in the fiery furnace, scared that they would lose their life because they loved God. They didn't see a way out of the fiery furnace, but God walked with them. They didn't know how, but they knew God.

Job—that was a tricky one. He lost everything he had, his wife started talking crazy, sickness ailed his body, he went broke, and he lost all his children. But in spite of that, Job knew that he came into this world with nothing and he can't leave with anything. Job didn't understand, but one thing's for sure: he knew God.

I know God. I know what His word has declared over my life, and I know what He has said about me. I know that I'm victorious; I know I win; I know I'm loved; I know I'm redeemed; I know I'm saved; I know I'm delivered; I know God holds me close; and I know God cares for me.

There are many things I don't know, but one thing for sure: I know God. In knowing God, I have the majority; I know that there is more with me than against me (2 Kings 6:16). Because I know Him, I am more than a conqueror; because I know Him, I can live to faith it another day; because I know Him, I am powered, purposed, and justified. All because I know Him, I can stand.

I know what God has done before. I know what God has already delivered me from. I know what God has saved me from, and I know the ways He has already made for me.

I don't know how, but I know God. I pray this has blessed your spirit.

—Blessings Flow

ABOUT THE AUTHOR

Sharay Mungin Mosley was born and raised in Hollywood, South Carolina, where she was educated in the public schools of Charleston County. She is happily married to her loving husband, Kelvin Mosley, for nearly seven years. Over the years, she obtained her bachelor of science in business administration and a master's of science in professional accounting.

She's always had a passion for encouraging and inspiring individuals since college. This led to her love for blogging, which she's been doing for nearly ten years. Through her passion for blogging, Inside Your Dreams Inc. was founded in 2011. Through IYD, she continues to aspire, encourage, and motivate individuals to define their purpose and live their God-given dreams.

IYD Inc. was birthed from life lessons and godly teachings inspired by the Holy Spirit. She desires to share these intricate godly lessons with the masses, and thus this project was born. Through the help of the Holy Spirit, she presses forward to continue the work to inspire individuals, young and experienced, to dream…

CPSIA information can be obtained
at www.ICGtesting.com
Printed in the USA
BVHW080939310522
638501BV00009B/362